Prison Round Trip

BY KLAUS VIEHMANN

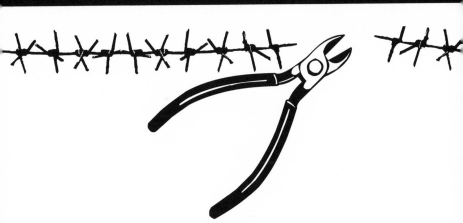

PREFACE BY BILL DUNNE
INTRODUCTION BY GABRIEL KUHN

PM Press Pamphlet Series

PM PRESS PAMPHLET SERIES No. 0007

PRISON ROUND TRIP
By Klaus Viehmann

PREFACE BY BILL DUNNE
INTRODUCTION BY GABRIEL KUHN
TRANSLATION BY GABRIEL KUHN
FOOTNOTES TO PRISON ROUND TRIP BY KLAUS VIEHMANN FOR ENGLISH EDITION.

ISBN: 978-1-60486-082-5

PM PRESS
PO BOX 23912
OAKLAND, CA 94623
WWW.PMPRESS.ORG

KERSPLEBEDEB
CP 63560, CCCP VAN HORNE
MONTREAL, QUEBEC
CANADA H3W 3H8
WWW.KERSPLEBEDEB.COM

LAYOUT AND DESIGN: KERSPLEBEDEB

PRINTED IN OAKLAND, CA ON RECYCLED PAPER WITH SOY INK.

Nothing is more certain than that radical leftists working for a revolutionary replacement of the imperial capitalist paradigm will increasingly go to prison. The social, economic, political contradictions are sharpening; the tipping point approaches as competition from the developing world imposes on first world bourgeoisie a need to depress the living standards of the working class it exploits and oppresses. The repressive strategies used against revolutionary movements in third world countries, however, will not fly in the first world, at least not yet. Populations there are too steeped in the political mythology that governments of the "free" do not prey upon the citizenry and class war is a fiction of "outside agitators". Further, first world societies tend to be too well integrated for such wholesale predation as occurred in, say, Suharto's Indonesia or even Videla's Argentina to be adequately hidden until its work is done. Witness the recent defeats of Bush's reactionary U.S. administration regarding torture and killing of even non-citizens. Plus, the richer and more educated populations have greater capacity to resist their immiseration. Hence, prisons will be the leading edge of the repressive apparatus as the current ruling class seeks to maintain its hegemony by criminalizing, incapacitating, and intimidating its challengers.

Former political prisoner Klaus Viehmann spent 15 long times jousting with the German state in its maximum security prisons after his capture as a practitioner of armed struggle. From that vantage, he lays out a strategy and tactical examples for continuing the struggle for the most equitable social reality in a prison environment—and, in so doing, surviving the oppression politically intact. And he correctly asserts that this is THE task: succumbing to a replacement consciousness imposed by a bourgeois state is tantamount to political and therefore personal death, whatever the residual corporeal state. In addition, Klaus shows that the rigors of surviving prison as an instrument of political repression hold lessons for people beyond the dark concrete corners and razor wire thickets that somewhat arbitrarily define the boundary between fettered and free.

Every person who aspires to revolutionary status has an obligation to struggle in whatever community s/he finds him or herself. Klaus shows that in this obligation is the key to surviving imprisonment. Prison is a de facto community. Seeking out comrades, friends, and potential comrades and friends—both within and without the durance vile—with whom to contest the authoritarian status quo in however limited a manner—is good advice. Sometimes this may involve direct and furious action; more usually it entails reading and writing and otherwise communicating. This resistance is what maintains a political consciousness that might otherwise be bled and squeezed into unrecognizability. While dreaming and fantasizing and speculating as a strictly cerebral activity may be diverting and useful in formulating a vision of the future we would build, they are not enough by themselves. Verily, they can be a debilitating distraction. Their results must be tested against the vagaries of empirical reality and the conclusions of others. Praxis is, after all, the unity of thought and action.

Part of this unification is overt resistance to the agency of repression via direct action, but the bigger part is maintaining and improving the implements of emancipation. Klaus pictures how this may be done by actively and passively opposing encroachments on prisoners' retained and contested rights where possible and by filling the vast bulk of time where that is not happening with reading, writing, and otherwise interacting with people both within the prison and across its barriers.

Moreover, Klaus explains that we cannot just ride with the tide and go with the flow. An isolated prisoner will find that relating to the world solely according to the norms of the prison administration and whatever bourgeois media it might make available—or even only through the norms of the criminal element characteristic of prison populations—will result in the analysis and attitudes thereof insinuating themselves into consciousness without vigilant efforts to contextualize or exclude them. Not relating to the world, merely wallowing in assumed misery, is even worse.

Conditions, time, and place always govern the mode of struggle. Klaus explores how in prison, where the power relations are so asymmetric, this means we must pick our fights and that there is "no absolutely correct way of acting". Today's effective action might be tomorrow's counterproductive debacle. Jurisdictions vary widely in what is possible and what may be fatal, as Klaus's contrast of German political imprisonment with that of past Latin American military dictatorships and nazi gulags illustrates. Even now, prison conditions and practicable political action within them vary markedly across first world jurisdictions, let alone the rest of the world.

Socio-political survival strategies within and without prisons may not necessarily mean individual physical survival. Klaus raises the RAF hunger strikes—and their tragic deaths—as examples: they drew the prisoners together and made them more conscious of their identity and strength and mobilized outside support that otherwise may have flagged. The apparatus retreated in the face of such solidarity. The hunger strikes of the IRA prisoners and their martyrdom worked similarly, as are the death fasts of Turkish political prisoners against F-type (isolation) prisons now. Class war, like any other, will have casualties; risk is an unavoidable element of life and struggle.

Sometimes a prisoner must precipitate the contradiction—barricade the cell and refuse a diminution of his or her circumstances, that being a losing proposition notwithstanding; physically resist an injustice, consequences assumed; sabotage the prison or forced labor or organize the strike, wagering whatever penalties; try the perimeter, chancing apparatus gunmen; file the grievance, writ, law suit, despite their connection to "diesel therapy"[1] and other retaliation. Sometimes losses happen on the best analysis, and sometimes the results of such actions turn out better for the group than the individual. Nevertheless, they are often demanded by principle and/or analysis and turn out well worth the tax because they roll the struggle forward and the apparatus back. Such deeds also inhibit agents of repression from selecting their doers as people who will acquiesce to the next increment of oppression and make it easier to impose on subsequent victims.

That the personal is political is axiomatic on the left. Everything is political. Klaus informs us that we must not allow the prison regimen to focus us unduly on the personal, make us see the world (and our imprisonment) in terms of self, make us, in Klaus's word, egotistical. He lyrically tells us, "True survival means to experience yourself as a human being who is socially, politically, mentally, and emotionally autonomous and self responsible. This requires breaking your isolation... .Those who cannot transcend their own imprisonment...will be unable to find meaning in their arduous situation." Only through connecting with a social infrastructure via such transcendence can we both sow and reap the liberation

---

1 A reference to the practice of bussing politically active and otherwise disruptive prisoners around the country, holding them in different prisons for short periods of time, effectively disrupting their social relationships and cutting them off from supporters, friends, and family.

that builds in a sociological feedback loop of synthesizing the personal and political.

Each of us has just a single, finite life, and its youth is but a fleeting commutation. That can make the prospect of a 10, 20, 30 year, or life sentence exceedingly threatening and daunting. Klaus reveals, however, that such apparent doom is an avoidable matter of perception. Don't dwell on the passage of time, we learn, use it; time is our most valuable resource. Just because we'd rather be doing something else doesn't mean there's nothing to do. Don't pine for the blandishments of the outer world! Live life! We don't "miss" life in prison, we just have a different one to lead— as we would have if any of a number of things had happened instead of arrest. Use that life to read, write, study, learn; on the basis of being free to do that, we can teach as well. Even if the interaction is so little as with authors and unsendable writing, it is work and connection and valuable— life. This is, as Klaus says, the most important advice.

Develop a broader, deeper, more durable understanding of why we seek revolution to increase the likelihood of achieving it. Maintain and hone the tools of the struggle and improve facility with them. A book, a magazine, a newspaper is a sawn bar, a cut fence, a hole in the wall, at least for a time. Learn how to do something material—electricity, welding, mechanics, computers—whatever. We are material beings in a material world, and knowing how to manipulate material will also raise the probability of achieving revolution. And on material, don't neglect the body, the most basic tool of struggle. It cannot be disparaged as merely the meat; the mind and the body are symbiotes, both essential elements of our potentially revolutionary beings. Exercise can be done in virtually any circumstances. Nor is exercise strictly physical; it is therapy, and it steals time back from the apparatus.

Communication is the thing out of which all other action grows. This is inherent and the core in Klaus's advocacy of reading, writing, and interacting. In order to be the autonomous, self-responsible person within and to and for the social relation of a revolutionary movement and act accordingly, communication is inescapable. We are and will be only as effective as our communication, internal and external. Our ability to read and learn and understand and even act from the experience of others and to communicate that knowledge, preferably refined through our own praxis, is what lets us advance social liberation. Klaus's take on survival strategy tells us we can not only survive thusly but can as well continue to serve the cause of liberation—which are really the same thing. We can be captured without giving in or giving up.

I cannot comment from experience on Klaus's rendition of how surviving thusly will facilitate the sea change to lower security existence on the streets, not having made that transition. But I am still here and I am still curious, as Klaus says a stir survivor will be. So I assume his conclusion is also correct that "there is life after survival and it is still worth living".

Bill Dunne
USP Big Sandy
20 November 2008

Bill Dunne was captured on October 14, 1979. He had been shot three times by police, and according to the state had been involved in an attempt to break a comrade out of the Seattle jail, as part of an unnamed anarchist collective. In 1980, he received a ninety-five-year sentence, and in 1983 had a consecutive fifteen years with five concurrent added due to an attempted escape. As he has stated, "The aggregate 105 years is a 'parole when they feel like it' sort of sentence."

"Prison Round Trip" was first published in German in 2003 as "Einmal Knast und zurück." The essay's author, Klaus Viehmann, had been released from prison ten years earlier, after completing a 15-year sentence for his involvement in urban guerilla activities in Germany in the 1970s. "Einmal Knast und zurück" first appeared in *Arranca!*, a journal founded 1993—coincidentally the year of Viehmann's release—to encourage critical debate within radical left and autonomist circles. The essay was subsequently reprinted in various forums. It is a reflection on prison life and on how to keep one's sanity and political integrity within the hostile and oppressive prison environment. In line with the *Arranca!* issue it was written for, "survival strategies" are its central theme.

"Einmal Knast und zurück" soon found an audience extending beyond Germany's borders. Thanks to translations by comrades and radical distribution networks, it has since been eagerly discussed amongst political prisoners from Spain to Greece. This is the first time the text is available to a wider English-speaking audience.

Klaus Viehmann grew up in Germany's industrial heartland, the Ruhr River Valley. He was politicized in the context of the late 1960s antiestablishment rebellions. In 1972, he moved to West Berlin in order to avoid military service, as residents of the city were exempt from the draft during Germany's division following World War II. Viehmann has cited the military coup in Chile in September 1973 as a pivotal event in his political development. In his words, the overthrow of the Allende government "destroyed the last illusions about a 'peaceful transition to socialism.'" As a consequence, the urban guerilla struggle seemed "much more plausible" than it had before.[1]

In 1975, Viehmann established contact with the 2nd of June Movement *(Bewegung 2. Juni)*, one of four major urban guerilla groups that emerged in Germany in the 1970s and 1980s, the others being the Red Army Faction *(Rote Armee Fraktion)*, the Revolutionary Cells *(Revolutionäre Zellen)*, and the Rote Zora.[2]

---

1 Klaus Viehmann, "Stadtguerilla und Klassenkampf—revised," in: *jour fixe initiative berlin* (ed.): Klassen und Kämpfe, Münster: Unrast 2006, p. 72.
2 For more on these four groups see: André Moncourt and J. Smith, "West Germany's Guerillas: Overview," http://www.germanguerilla.com/overview.html

The Red Army Faction (RAF) was the first and most enduring of these groups and remains the most legendary. Spectacular actions throughout the 1970s brought far-reaching attention, a dedicated circle of sympathizers, and effective martial law in Germany. With the unresolved prison death of the so-called First Generation's most prominent members, the RAF experienced a strong blow in the fall of 1977. However, the group remained active for another twenty years, before it finally disbanded in 1998.

Where the RAF had shaped a Marxist-Leninist and increasingly anti-imperialist ideology in a series of theoretical documents, the second of West Germany's urban guerilla groups, the West Berlin-based 2nd of June Movement (2JM), was committed to anti-authoritarian principles and served to give armed expression to everyday struggles. Formed in January 1972, its members were drawn from radical grassroots and community groups, including both students and workers.

The Revolutionary Cells (RZ), a group with its roots in the undogmatic left, announced its existence in 1973. The RZ soon divided into a "social revolutionary" and an "anti-imperialist" wing. The latter collaborated with guerilla groups operating in an international context, mainly from the Middle East, and its involvement in high-level hostage-takings and sky-jackings outside of West Germany would prove extremely controversial. On the other hand, the social revolutionary wing, made up of members who remained active aboveground, would carry out numerous, often low-level, actions in connection with popular struggles of the day, achieving an enviable level of support on the left.

If the social revolutionary wing of the RZ was popular, this was arguably even more the case for the Rote Zora, a women's guerilla group that grew out of the RZ. Largely concentrating on issues central to women's struggles, the Rote Zora would play its most influential role through a 1980s campaign of actions directed at gene tech and biotechnology.

Both the Revolutionary Cells and Rote Zora ended their activities in 1993.

Klaus Viehmann was arrested in West Berlin in 1978, charged with membership in the 2JM and a number of related activities, including bank robbery and the liberation of prisoners, and sentenced to 15 years in prison.

Viehmann was one of the 2JM members who were opposed to any collaboration that threatened the group's autonomy—this concerned an anti-imperialist alliance with international guerilla movements as much as closer ties to the Red Army Faction. The involvement of German guerillas in the hijacking of passenger planes proved particularly divisive within the group. Eventually, the conflict led to a split in 1980 when some members joined the Red Army Faction, while Viehmann and others did not. This marked the end of the 2JM as an active group. Viehmann subsequently emphasized his long-standing affinity for the social revolutionary wing of the Revolutionary Cells.

While still in prison, Viehmann wrote an essay that became the centerpiece of the book *Drei zu Eins* ("Three to One"), published in 1991. The book introduced the concept of "triple oppression"—the interrelations between class, gender and race in oppressive social structures—to a radical German-speaking audience, and proved highly influential, especially in autonomist circles.

Since his release, Viehmann has been active in various left-wing projects, including solidarity campaigns for World War II forced laborers and Colombian trade unionists. He remains involved in numerous publishing activities, as an author, translator, and a graphic designer. He is also co-editor of two extensive volumes documenting the history of autonomist political poster art in Germany: *hoch die kampf dem* (1999) and *vorwärts bis zum nieder mit* (2001). His home is once again Berlin—today officially undivided, but, as he puts it, "a place where a lot needs to be done."

Gabriel Kuhn is an Austrian-born writer and translator. He is the founder of Alpine Anarchist Productions (www.alpineanarchist.org) and has published widely on radical theory, culture and politics. For PM Press he has authored *Life Under the Jolly Roger: Reflections on Golden Age Piracy* (2009), edited *Sober Living for the Revolution: Hardcore Punk, Straight Edge, and Radical Politics* (2010), and translated Gustav Landauer's *Revolution and Other Writings: A Political Reader* (2010).

Photo of Klaus Viehmann during a lineup
a few weeks after his arrest in 1978.

Bang. The door to your cell is shut. You have survived the arrest, you are mad that you weren't more careful, you worry that they will get others too, you wonder what will happen to your group and whether a lawyer has been called yet—of course you show none of this. The weapon, the fake papers, your own clothes, all gone. The prison garb and the shoes they've thrown at you are too big—maybe because they want to play silly games with you, maybe because they really blow "terrorists" out of proportion in their minds—and the control over your own appearance taken out of your hands. You look around, trying to get an understanding of where you'll spend the next few years of your life.

What is the point of talking about survival strategies today—years later? Is it worth trying to organize and sum up your experiences? It is, at any rate, difficult to bring them into words and sentences. Yet, for those who will spend time behind bars in the future, they might be useful. Besides, since the experiences of (political) prisoners are neither extra-societal nor a-historical, their survival strategies might also help those comrades who experience their everyday life as little more than a somewhat coordinated form of "getting by." To focus on what's essential, to plan your everyday life consciously, to use your energies in meaningful ways—these are all qualities that are useful. Everywhere. Survival strategies are personal (which is why this text is, also rhetorically, directed at you, no abstract third person), but not egotistical. Emancipation and liberation do not happen within the individual—they are socio-historical processes. In the words of Peter Brückner,[1] "It was only the late bourgeois who has turned freedom and independence into a question of 'inwardness.'" This shows the limits

---

1 Social psychologist and psychoanalyst; popular left-wing university professor, sympathizer of Germany's extra-parliamentary opposition; accused of supporting the RAF in 1972, and temporarily suspended from his post.

of all individual survival strategies. Surviving can only turn into living through social liberation. But this is another story, one in which prisons will hardly play a role...

In prison, the necessity of survival strategies is immediate; without them you are at the mercy of the enemy. Prison is a hostile environment, and it has been designed as such by people who see you as their foe. Have no illusions about that. In regular prisons—especially old-fashioned ones—conditions are often atrocious and sometimes violent, but there are at least social structures. In isolation or maximum security units, social relations are controlled, regulated, abolished. Isolation means the absence of social life and the presence of yourself. You have nothing but yourself, and you have to find ways to deal with it. This is possible, but it is not possible to know beforehand who will get through prison okay and who won't. For someone with little life experience, limited political self-motivation and uncertain (possibly egotistical) future plans, it will be difficult. A colorful biography in which prison does not mark the first rough period, optimism even in the face of a dire situation and the ability not to take yourself too seriously all help.

Ernst Bloch[1] might have said that "those who acquire their knowledge only from books should be put onto shelves," but it is not necessarily a tragedy if the knowledge about certain things only comes that way. I have not experienced physical torture, death threats or confinement in dark cells. Personal or literary descriptions of such experiences, however, can help you to understand your own experiences better and to get through them.

The empirical basis (if you will) for this text is 15 years imprisonment. Seven years—after 1978—were spent in isolation or with small groups of inmates, five of these in maximum security units (in Moabit and Bielefeld). From 1986 until my release in 1993, I was in a special "security cell" in Werl, an old German prison. I had one hour in the yard every day with other inmates. My visits and my mail was monitored, I was separated from my lawyers by a bulletproof glass window, I was hardly ever allowed to buy extra supplies, had no visits of other prisoners in my cell, showered alone, was allowed a maximum of 30 books, no radio and five or six subscriptions to newspapers and magazines. Mail restrictions were eased during my last years there, and from 1991 to 1993 I was permitted to jog

---

1   Popular left-wing philosopher propagating "concrete utopias" and "the principle of hope."

in the yard twice a week. What I am writing here is the quintessence of my experiences. During the first five or six years of my imprisonment, I learned the survival strategies that got me through the last ten. These are the experiences I'm summarizing here.

Back to the first day in prison. You have no conception of the day you will be released. 5,500 days are beyond what is imaginable, even when I look back at it. What you see at the time is what you need to know to survive right there and then: Where do I get reading and writing material? Where do I hide secret messages? When should I expect a cell search? Where are the cells of my comrades? There is a lot to do. Boredom is the least of your concerns. Besides, you know why you are in there—an enormous advantage compared to those who have no idea. It was a radical political challenge that got you there; one that you could see as "just another step" in a life that you had chosen by engaging in militant left-wing politics. Sure, they were one up on you at that point, but prison was a new terrain and they still had to prove that they could break you. This is exactly what you must not allow them to do—and this, in turn, defines your struggle from the first day to the last.

To have a clear objective and clear front lines enables you to fight well. You must never allow them to persuade you that there are no clear front lines and that "big brother" is your friend. Ulrike Meinhof's[1] declaration that "the fight of the people against power is the fight of remembering against forgetting" sums this up perfectly. The ability to remember requires political and/or moral conviction. Those who lose this conviction refuse to remember and get lost in self-reflection, self-pity and lack of orientation. This is the steep decline where desperation can turn into suicide and political denial into betrayal. Solitary confinement and the control of social contact (letters, visits, news), you can also call it brainwashing, aim at causing you to forget and to become egotistical. Resistance,

---

1 Left-wing journalist, co-founder of the RAF in 1970; the reasons for her death in Stammheim Prison in 1975 remain unresolved.

solidarity, responsibility, collectivism and a corresponding personality shall vanish.

Maximum security prisons also follow the bourgeois-capitalist principle of "everyone is his/her own best friend." Those who adopt this principle do not survive—they turn into someone else. Not because they grew and achieved emancipation, but because they regressed and de-socialized. The consequences are de-politicization and the disintegration of the personality. True survival means to experience yourself as a human being who is socially, politically, mentally and emotionally autonomous and self-responsible. This requires breaking your isolation and finding reference points outside your cell. Those who cannot transcend their own imprisonment and who cannot understand it in a wider context will be unable to find meaning in their arduous situation. The narrower your horizon, the more paralyzing and desperate your personal fears. Jean Amery[1] once described these "reference points" in connection with the most extreme of all experiences, that of Auschwitz:

> *"You must realize," a religious Jew once told me, "that your intelligence and education is worthless here. Me, however, I know that God will take revenge." A German leftist comrade, in the camp since 1933, expressed this more bluntly: "There you are, you bourgeois know-it-alls, and you shiver when the SS appears. We do not shiver, and even if we will perish in here miserably, we know that the comrades who follow us will line them all up." Both these men transcended themselves and projected themselves into the future. ... Their belief or their ideology gave them a stable point in the world that allowed them to spiritually defy the SS-State.*

Günter Anders[2] has called this the "paradox of hopelessness creating hope."

In the much less dangerous world of West German high security prisons, it is rare that your physical survival is threatened. There is enough food, clothing, warmth and hygiene—an enormous difference from the conditions in, for example, military prisons in Latin America. Despite such differences, however, you have to figure out how to survive with your

---

1 Jewish author, resistance fighter, and Auschwitz survivor; committed suicide in 1978.
2 Social philosopher and radical pacifist; emphasized the necessity to resist even under the most desperate conditions.

personality intact. How do you protect yourself? How do you organize your defense? And when do you have to attack? The first impulse of course says: *Always!* But to act politically means to assess power balances and the consequences of your actions—also in prison. For example, there is no point in destroying your cell if no one on the outside will ever know about it. It might be fun, sure, but it will almost certainly cause time in the hole and repercussions. However, when in 1980 the first prisoners were meant to be transferred to the newly constructed maximum security unit in Moabit,[1] it made sense to barricade yourself behind the dismantled furniture of your cell. This showed that you refused to go to this unit voluntarily, that you refused to accept a worsening of your conditions without resistance. If you do not show such resistance it will make them overconfident and you will feel powerless in your new surroundings. In the case of Moabit, comrades protested on the outside, there were militant actions and the media coverage was huge. For surviving the maximum security conditions, this was all extremely helpful.

The hunger strikes of the 1970s and 1980s were—despite the critique of their exact circumstances and certain demands—"survival strategies" for prisoners in isolation and maximum security units. The solidarity campaigns that followed the deaths of Holger Meins and Sigurd Debus[2]— killed by medical negligence and force feeding—definitely helped the survival of their imprisoned comrades. Here is an example for an immediate survival strategy from my own experience: In 1983, the authorities intended to implement a new model of isolating small groups of prisoners in the maximum security unit in Bielefeld. It was planned to supplement the maximum security architecture with an extremely rigid regime: for a dirty sink, you would lose three days in the yard, turning off the common room's idiotic, prison-selected TV program meant confinement to your cell for two weeks, etc. Forced labor programs were added to this: assembling 3,000 clothespins in an eight-hour workday, five days a week, under CCTV surveillance, with disciplinary measures for poor output. The enforcement of repetitive and mind-numbing activities is essential in all psychological conditioning, a classic means of brainwashing directed at the body. To assemble clothespins for years equals a slow mental death.

---

1   One of West Germany's biggest prisons, built from 1877 to 1882 by French prisoners of war; extended under the Nazi regime.
2   RAF prisoners; both died in connection with a prisoners' hunger strike: Holger Meins due to a lack of medical attention in 1974; Sigurd Debus due to force-feeding in 1981.

Punishment for work refusal was the hole. Since a hunger strike (possibly of several weeks) is difficult under such circumstances, and since everything seemed at stake anyway, the only available means was a thirst strike. Thirst strikes do not last long—one way or another. Public pressure has to be mounted fast, and this pressure has to become stronger than, in this case, their interest in implementing the new maximum security forced labor model. The survival strategy in this case was to challenge them to explain why 3,000 clothespins a day were worth a human being's death. Besides, there was an unspoken, yet clear, understanding that if they did implement forced labor within the maximum security units, attacks on the prison labor system would become so strong that it would be impossible to maintain prison labor even in the regular units, which would have caused substantial loss of income. They gave in after five days, having suffered significant property damage: the Revolutionary Cells (*Revolutionäre Zellen*, RZ) had bombed the prison bureau and the offices of two companies profiting from prison labor. Added to this were demonstrations, a riot in the maximum security unit in Köln-Ossendorf and bad press. Since then, no further attempt has ever been made to implement forced labor in maximum security facilities.

Most times, however, the life of a prisoner is less heroic. After all, the natural enemy of the hero is daily routine. Here is an example, though, of a tiny survival strategy: If your request to see the prison dentist remains "overlooked" for two days, you can tape it to the toilet which can then be demounted and, at the next opportunity, placed in front of your cell— just so it won't be "overlooked" any longer. This will lead to some money being taken from the solidarity account and will result in a disciplinary measure, but you will see the dentist. Such an action works because the denial of dental services becomes official with the property damage which needs to be registered. This means you will have the option of filing a legal complaint—something that the prison administration usually does not want to deal with in such petty cases.

Of course you cannot rattle your bars or kick against your door all day. You won't be able to keep that up for very long. However, not being able to tear down the bars or to kick in the door does not mean that you have to accept the prison's regime and be forced into norms that are a lot narrower than those on the outside. You can keep your individuality only by resisting these norms. Live or be lived. An acceptance of the norms means an end to your own development. You lose interest in social contact and refuse to accept that circumstances and situations change. To adapt to the prison regime means to forget individual strength and success. The adaptation reproduces itself endlessly, both because you fear the actual regime and the personal consequences of resistance. You lose hope. Eventually, accepting the wrongs turns into embracing the rules. Not only optimism is dependent on activity, resistance is too. Being lethargic makes you dumb. Merely thinking about resistance (what the Nazi pawns called "inner emigration") is no survival strategy; it is cynicism: you think one thing, but you do another; or you refuse to draw the consequences of your thoughts.

The praxis of imagined resistance has a name: expected behavior. When you are passive you internalize fear and hopelessness. This creates—and reproduces—the obedient, neurotic prisoner. This prisoner's daydreams about spectacular escapes or unexpected pardons fall under the authority-sanctioned category of "Give-us-our-daily-illusion." Within the "false life" of prison there can be no absolutely correct ways of acting. However, fundamental decisions about your actions can still be made—decisions that are an important part of your survival strategies. They are not dogmatic. They have to be revised again and again. Is it wrong to give in? Are the old principles still valid? You always have to know this; you always have to convince yourself anew. Your responses must not just be habits. You ought to be curious and open when it comes to the experiences and perspectives of others, and you ought to appreciate friendly advice.

To make clear decisions on the basis of your memories and your knowledge, while accepting contradictions and acknowledging the change of social and political realities, in other words, to think dialectically, is a solid basis for your own conviction. Rigid and inflexible thinking can only make an exterior frame that does not even allow for the tiniest of cracks. If one detail seems off, everything seems off... This is why it is such tiny cracks that can sometimes cause those who once professed a "150%" conviction to crumble. The next thing they do is to look for a new framework. Not one that necessarily makes much sense, but one that might lead to an earlier release. Look at the example of Horst Mahler[1]: after a lot of ideological meandering, he finally settled on the far right when, after studying the relevant literature extensively, he came to the brash conclusion in the late 1970s that Marx had misunderstood Hegel and that we all ought to reconsider our understanding of the State. In a *Spiegel* interview,[2] he managed to outdo even the Minister of the Interior in his praise for the State institution. He was released early.

Of course, you will develop politically, reflect on the political praxis you were engaged in before you went to prison, etc. Yet, dialectical thinking will only foster your conviction that exploitation, oppression, poverty and war will not disappear without the overthrow of the prevailing order. This is what will always separate you from a Minister of the Interior.

The question of whether it is "wrong to give in" can be put into simple terms: Do you want to talk to someone who locks you up during the day and who is ready to shoot you if you attempt to escape during the night? Do you want to talk to the head of a prison who prohibits any commemoration of those who, in 1943, were sent to die in Mauthausen from the very yard you walk in every day? Or do you want to talk with the one who attends military training as a "reserve captain"? Do you want to strike a deal with the Federal Criminal Bureau (*Bundeskriminalamt*, BKA), an organization maintaining a department called "TE"[3] (formerly *"Sicherheitsgruppe Bonn"* and established by former officials of the Nazis' Reich Security Head Office (*Reichssicherheitshauptamt*)) that spies on your visitors and was involved in the death of Wolfgang Grams?[4] Do you want to bow in front of them in exchange for nothing more than a few perks? The "reason" that they demand of you rocks the cradle of both madness and betrayal, and the "common sense" they evoke "is the little man in the grey suit who never makes a mistake in addition—but it's always someone else's money he's adding up." (Raymond Chandler)

---

1 Lawyer in support of the students' rebellion, co-founder of the RAF; distanced himself from the armed struggle three years later and joined first the KPD/AO, a Marxist-Leninist student group, then the FDP, Germany's main "liberal" party, and finally the NPD, a neofascist party.
2 *Der Spiegel* is a widely read German weekly, notorious for its "antiterrorist" stance.
3 TE = "terrorism."
4 In 1993 there was a shoot-out at a German small town train station between RAF members and a special unit of the German police. One policeman died, Wolfgang Grams was badly injured; according to the police report, Grams then committed suicide, while witnesses claim that he was shot dead by a policeman from close range.

It is sweet but dangerous to wait for letters...
to lay awake till the morning and stare at the ceiling...
Forget your age, beware of the spring evenings...
It is bad to dream of roses and gardens,
    but good to think of mountains and oceans.
My advice to you would be: read and write as much as possible—
    and ignore the mirror

Nazim Hikmet[1]
letter to a fellow prisoner

Nazim Hikmet's lines express pure survival strategies. Letters are important fractures in the prison walls, but to focus on receiving them makes you dependent. Be happy when they arrive—look for something else to be happy about when they don't. To lie awake until morning and stare at the ceiling does not change anything. To read and write until morning, however, might, as it means that you are active. To forget one's age and the mirror eradicates the worries about missing out on life. Beautiful spring evenings can cause terrible yearning for the world outside. To dream of roses and gardens appeases you in a place where you shouldn't be appeased. To think of untamed mountains and seas puts your own problems into perspective. To read and write as much as possible is the most crucial advice; in the long term, this is the most important requirement of each and every survival strategy in prison.

Books can take you to a different world when the one you are facing is intolerable. They allow you to travel even though you are trapped. This is of inestimable value in solitary confinement. Besides, it helps your survival strategies in the long run to engage with thoughts and people through reading and writing. It might be difficult against the backdrop

---

1   Popular Turkish communist poet, died in Russian exile in 1963.

of the exhausting monotony of prison, but it is the precondition for you to be engaged. Being engaged means new social relationships and new thoughts that keep you alive. Nobody wants to hear the same stories from you year after year, about shoot-outs or eternal truths or your problems inside. The Salvation Army might want to listen to your laments, but nobody who sees you as a political subject will.

Once you have managed to resist repression during your first months and years of prison, time becomes your main enemy. Physically you can stay fit—you can exercise even in a prison cell, and cigarettes, coffee and sweets are too expensive anyway. The sheer length of the years, however, affects the possibilities of creating a life trajectory, of experiencing life as a whole—something that forms an identity. It is difficult to understand your own patterns of behavior as coherent and meaningful. On the outside, you can be relatively certain in your knowledge that you are a person who—despite developing, of course—is always the same person, with his or her interests, ideas, reasoning and self-confidence. Now you always have to check your personality, your consciousness and your ability to think and see if all this hasn't somehow changed without you noticing. Without a rigorous self-reflection about your thoughts, emotions and actions, you cannot be certain that you still think and act rationally—something you could take for granted before.

"You can understand things by changing them," Bertolt Brecht said dialectically, and it is this praxis of realization that Nazim Hikmet describes above. To read Marx and Gramsci, Rosa Luxemburg and Assata Shakur, Malcolm X and Primo Levi, Vera Figner and Peter Weiss,[1] or to read about the history of the Peasant Wars or the Black Panthers, or about internationalism, natural sciences, art history or chess games—all this does not cut through the bars of your cell, but it helps you to preserve your ability to think and discuss. In the worst case, you can use the Bible as the only book allowed in the hole: "to open eyes that are blind, to free captives from prison and to release from the dungeon those who sit in darkness." (Isaiah 42: 7)

Reading is an active exchange of thoughts with others. Language is practical consciousness. Writing is production. Intellectual activity that does not result in communicable thoughts, i.e. in speaking or writing (for

---

1 Primo Levi, Italian author, antifascist, and Auschwitz survivor; Vera Figner, Russian social revolutionary, spent 20 years in prison due to her involvement in the assassination of Tsar Alexander II; Peter Weiss, German communist author, best known for *The Aesthetics of Resistance*.

others), turns, in the long run—not only in prison—into a Sisyphean task. You do not live and think and write on a mythical mountain, though, but in a specific social situation. In this case: in prison. You ought to be aware of the impact that the contradictions of your situation have on your thoughts. Certain essential political realizations might in fact come more easily with some distance from the hustle and bustle of everyday life, but you ought to be very careful with all evaluations that require sensual experience. ... In any case, it is the connection of your theoretical reflections to the current problems of the left, i.e., the problems of your comrades and friends on the outside, that gives your learning and writing a practical meaning—something that can get you through many years.

Bang. The door is shut again. This time, however, you are on the outside. This does not come as surprisingly as the arrest and is significantly more pleasant. It is similarly confusing, though. You spin around like a matchbox car. It takes awhile—and hitting a few corners—before you stop and are able to really take a good look around. Your prison survival strategies helped you deal with an environment that is not really suitable for human life. Now all the strategies that you internalized get in your way. The prison experience teaches you to keep what is important to yourself, not to reveal anything, not to make yourself vulnerable. On the outside this appears—to put it mildly—as being insensitive. Friends cannot understand your (lack of) reactions. Others—certainly not your friends—raise "ex-prisoners" onto pedestals that are, in fact, closets. It is neither uplifting nor a political program to have spent time in prison. The inevitably acquired ability to make decisions for yourself often leads to avoiding challenging collective discussions. Not wanting to be dependent on anything complicates possible bonds. The ability to be alone turns into a desire to be so. Your resistance to norms and your struggle to stay afloat as an individual now make you skeptical towards groups. After the seriousness of the prison experience, disputes within the left often appear irrelevant or even ridiculous—yet when you show this you appear arrogant. It is difficult to switch off the control over your emotions that you have worked so hard to attain, just so that they wouldn't be able to use your emotions against you. Love, hate, passion—everything is secured in an intellectual bag, and you look over your shoulder carefully before you untie anything. Sure, you keep misery away from you that way. But happiness too. With time, this becomes less severe. Things become easier. Still, what a former Tupamaro[1] described with the following words will stay with you:

> *You realize that one ... cannot live a lie comfortably without being disgusted by oneself, because you believe that those who understand but live inactively in comfort will break.*

In any case, there is life after survival, and it is worth living. Sean McGuffin's[2] comment that "age and trickery will always beat youth and strength" is as much a comfort to you as the useful degrees of persistence, patience and endurance that you could only acquire as a prisoner. You are still here, and you are still curious.

---

1 Tupamaros—*Movimiento de Liberación Nacional,* Uruguayan urban guerilla movement; active from 1963 into the 1970s.
2 Irish author and self-confessed "anarchist and intellectual rowdy"; imprisoned in the 1970s by the British Army for alleged IRA membership.

The Red Army Faction,
A Documentary History
Volume 1:
Projectiles For the People

Edited by J. Smith
and André Moncourt

Forewords by
Russell "Maroon" Shoats
and Bill Dunne

PM Press/Kersplebedeb
co-publication

736 pages paperback

ISBN: 978-1-60486-029-0

$34.95

For the first time ever in English, this volume presents all of the manifestos and communiqués issued by the Red Army Faction between 1970 and 1977, from Andreas Baader's prison break, through the 1972 May Offensive and the 1975 hostage-taking in Stockholm, to the desperate, and tragic, events of the "German Autumn" of 1977. The RAF's three main manifestos—*The Urban Guerilla Concept, Serve the People,* and *Black September*—are included, as are important interviews with *Spiegel* and *Le Monde Diplomatique,* and a number of communiqués and court statements explaining their actions.

Providing the background information that readers will require to understand the context in which these events occurred, separate thematic sections deal with the 1976 murder of Ulrike Meinhof in prison, the 1977 Stammheim murders, the extensive use of psychological operations and false-flag attacks to discredit the guerilla, the state's use of sensory deprivation torture and isolation wings, and the prisoners' resistance to this, through which they inspired their own supporters and others on the left to take the plunge into revolutionary action.

Drawing on both mainstream and movement sources, this book is intended as a contribution to the comrades of today—and to the comrades of tomorrow—both as testimony to those who struggled before and as an explanation as to how they saw the world, why they made the choices they made, and the price they were made to pay for having done so.

Let Freedom Ring:
A Collection of Documents from
the Movements to Free U.S.
Political Prisoners

Edited by Matt Meyer

Foreword by Nobel Peace
Laureate Adolfo Perez Esquivel

Afterwords by Ashanti Alston
and Lynne Stewart

PM Press/Kersplebedeb
co-publication

912 pages paperback

ISBN: 978-1-60486-035-1

$37.95

Let Freedom Ring presents a two-decade sweep of essays, analyses, histories, interviews, resolutions, People's Tribunal verdicts, and poems by and about the scores of U.S. political prisoners and the campaigns to safeguard their rights and secure their freedom. In addition to an extensive section on the campaign to free death-row journalist Mumia Abu-Jamal, represented here are the radical movements that have most challenged the U.S. empire from within: Black Panthers and other Black liberation fighters, Puerto Rican independentistas, Indigenous sovereignty activists, white anti-imperialists, environmental and animal rights militants, Arab and Muslim activists, Iraq war resisters, and others. Contributors in and out of prison detail the repressive methods—from long-term isolation to sensory deprivation to politically inspired parole denial—used to attack these freedom fighters, some still caged after 30+ years. This invaluable resource guide offers inspiring stories of the creative, and sometimes winning, strategies to bring them home.

With contributions by Mumia Abu-Jamal, Sundiata Acoli, Ramona Africa, Dan Berger, Dhoruba Bin-Wahad, Terry Bisson, B°, Marilyn Buck, Safiya Bukhari, Chrystos, Angela Davis, Susie Day, Bill Dunne, Jill Soffiyah Elijah, Bob Lederer, Jose López, Oscar López Rivera, Mairead Corrigan Maguire, Jalil Muntaqim, Luis Nieves Falcón, Leonard Peltier, Ninotchka Rosca, the San Francisco 8, Assata Shakur, Meg Starr, Jan Susler, Linda Thurston, Desmond Tutu, Laura Whitehorn, and many more…

PM Press was founded at the end of 2007 by a small collection of folks with decades of publishing, media, and organizing experience. PM co-founder Ramsey Kanaan started AK Press as a young teenager in Scotland almost 30 years ago and, together with his fellow PM Press co-conspirators, has published and distributed hundreds of books, pamphlets, CDs, and DVDs. Members of PM have founded enduring book fairs, spearheaded victorious tenant organizing campaigns, and worked closely with bookstores, academic conferences, and even rock bands to deliver political and challenging ideas to all walks of life. We're old enough to know what we're doing and young enough to know what's at stake.

We seek to create radical and stimulating fiction and non-fiction books, pamphlets, t-shirts, visual and audio materials to entertain, educate and inspire you. We aim to distribute these through every available channel with every available technology - whether that means you are seeing anarchist classics at our bookfair stalls; reading our latest vegan cookbook at the café; downloading geeky fiction e-books; or digging new music and timely videos from our website.

PM Press is always on the lookout for talented and skilled volunteers, artists, activists and writers to work with. If you have a great idea for a project or can contribute in some way, please get in touch.

PM Press . PO Box 23912 . Oakland CA 94623
510-658-3906
www.pmpress.org

Since 1998 Kersplebedeb has been an important source of radical literature and agit prop materials. The project has a non-exclusive focus on anti-patriarchal and anti-imperialist politics, framed within an anti-capitalist perspective. A special priority is given to writings regarding armed struggle in the metropole, and the continuing struggles of political prisoners and prisoners of war.

check it out on the web, or write for a free catalog:
kersplebedeb publishing and distribution
CP 63560, CCCP Van Horne, Montreal, Quebec, Canada, H3W 3H8
http://www.kersplebedeb.com • info@kersplebedeb.com
new website: www.leftwingbooks.net